Chambers Common Errors in Written English

Sarah Marriott
and
Barry Farrell

Chambers

EDINBURGH   NEW YORK

Published 1992 by W & R Chambers Ltd,
43–45 Annandale Street, Edinburgh EH7 4AZ
Reprinted 1993

British Library Cataloguing in Publication Data

A catalogue record for this book is available from the
British Library

ISBN 0-550-18046-X

Typeset by Chatsworth Studios Ltd,
Newcastle upon Tyne
Printed in England by Cox & Wyman Ltd, Reading

Introduction

What is the difference between **principle** and **principal**? Or **imply** and **infer**? Or **continuous** and **continual**? Is **criteria** singular or plural? How many **s**'s are there in **assistant**? Or **professor**? Where exactly should you put a comma? Or an apostrophe? *Common Errors in Written English* contains the answers to these questions, and to many more.

This book is intended for anyone who wants to write correct English. It includes entries on common spelling mistakes (and shows the differences between British and American spelling); simple punctuation rules; clear explanations of common grammatical errors; and advice on appropriate structures and vocabulary for formal writing.

Common Errors in Written English is a handy reference guide which is easy to use. Entries are arranged alphabetically, with explanations, examples of correct usage and, where helpful, of typical errors (preceded by an asterisk*).

A

a/an

(1) The form **a** is used with words and abbreviations which:

    a)   begin with a consonant:

    a contract   a hotel   a BBC programme   a NATO summit

    b)   are pronounced as though they begin with a consonant:

    a unit a usage manual   a one-way street   a UFO

(2) The form **an** is used before words and abbreviations which:

    a)   begin with a vowel:

    an orange   an accident   an EC summit   an IOU

    b)   are pronounced as though they begin with a vowel:

    an hour   an honour   an MP   an SOS

abbreviations

In modern British English **abbreviations** are often written without full stops, particularly where the abbreviated form is more widely used than the complete word(s):

Dr Newton	*the BBC*	*the UK*	*the USA*
5km	*ie*	*PTO*	*etc*

-able/-ible

The spelling of these two word-endings is often confused. There is no clear spelling rule, but note that **-able** is more widely used than **-ible**.

(1) Some common words with **-able** endings:

adaptable	*fashionable*	*preferable*	*shockable*
detachable	*indefinable*	*reliable*	*transferable*
drinkable	*payable*	*respectable*	*unmistakable*

When **-able** is added to a word ending in one *e*, that *e* is usually dropped:

    use/usable   advise/advisable   debate/debatable

Exceptions:

(a)   The *e* is not dropped when the word ends in *-ce* or *-ge*:

> *knowledge/knowledgeable   notice/noticeable*

(b)   In some words, both forms are acceptable; the forms listed below are the most common:

blameable	*livable*	*movable*	*shapable*
likeable	*lovable*	*rateable*	*sizeable*

(2)   Some common words ending in **-ible:**

accessible	*discernible*	*gullible*	*responsible*
compatible	*eligible*	*legible*	*reversible*
comprehensible	*feasible*	*negligible*	*inintelligible*
convertible	*flexible*	*permissible*	*visible*

abscess
Often misspelt. Note: *sc* in the middle, and *ss* at the end.

absence   see **lack.**

absorb/absorption
The verb is spelt with *b* but in the noun form this changes to *p*.

accent marks
The English language often 'takes over' words from other languages, and once they become widely accepted, their accent marks can be dropped:

> *café/cafe   paté/pate   détente/detente*

accommodation
Frequently misspelt. Remember: double *c* followed by *o* and then double *m* followed by *o*.

acquiesce
Note the spelling: *acq* at the beginning, and *sce* at the end.
Also, take care with the preposition following **acquiesce:**

> *He acquiesced in our proposals.*
> Not **acquiesced to*

Acquiesce is rather formal. For a more neutral style, use **agree (to).**

-acy/-asy

The spelling of these word-endings is often confused. Note that **-acy** is more widely used.

(1) Some common words ending in **-acy**:

accuracy	conspiracy	diplomacy	pharmacy
aristocracy	delicacy	allacy	privacy
bureaucracy	democracy	intimacy	supremacy

Note: many words ending in **-acy** are related to words ending in -at or -ate.

(2) Some common words ending in **-asy**:

ecstasy	fantasy	idiosyncrasy

adopted/adoptive

Adopted is often used where **adoptive** would be more accurate:

If Robin Phillips adopts Michael, Robin is Michael's adoptive father, and Michael is Robin's adopted son.

adverse see **averse**.

advice/advise

These two words are often used incorrectly in written English.

(1) **Advice** is a noun:
He gave me advice on cooking roast beef.
I gave him advice on how to make gravy.

(2) **Advise on** is a verb meaning 'to give advice to':
He advised me on cooking roast beef.
I advised him on how to make gravy.

(3) **Advise** + infinitive, and **advise** + -ing, mean 'recommend':
He advised me to cook chicken, instead of beef.
I advised making wine sauce, instead of gravy.

(4) In formal English **advise** means 'inform':
She advised them that the contract was not valid.
Please advise my solicitor of your intentions.

Aegean Sea

Note the spelling: *ae* at the beginning, and *ea* later.

affect see **effect**.

afflict   see **inflict**.

agenda

Originally **agenda** was the plural of **agendum**. However, in modern usage, **agenda** is used as a singular noun, and the plural is **agendas**.

agree with/to/on

(1) **Agree with** can mean 'to be, or come to be of one mind':

He agreed with her suggestion/explanation/idea etc.

It can also be used in the sense of 'to suit':

Wet weather does not agree with my grandfather.

(2) **Agree to** is used when 'a person will do or allow something':

She agreed to show us how to use the computer.

(3) One **agrees on** 'matter for decisions', usually after some discussion:

They agreed on the budget for the following year.

all ready/already

These are not synonymous.

(1) **All ready** means 'prepared':

The teacher was all ready to start the class.

(2) **Already** refers to a previous action:

I have already seen that film.

all right/alright

Alright is an unacceptable spelling of **all right.** Although often used, it remains incorrect.

all together/altogether

The two forms have different meanings.

(1) **All together** means 'in a group'. The two words may be separated:

I hate the paintings all together on that wall.
I hate all the paintings together on that wall.

(2) **Altogether** means 'completely' or 'in total':

He bought three books altogether.

allusion/illusion
(1) An **allusion** is an 'indirect reference':
He made an allusion to her weight.
This poem is full of allusions to the Bible.

(2) An **illusion** is a 'false conception or belief, often based on misleading evidence':
Anorexics have the illusion that they are fat.
Arthur thought he was a good student until his appalling exam results shattered his illusions.

already   see **all ready**.

alright   see **all right**.

also/as well/too
In written English, **also** is preferred as it is more formal. It should not be placed at the end of a sentence.

although/though
In a formal style, **although** is more usual than **though**. **Though** cannot be used to begin a sentence.

altogether   see **all together**.

amend   see **emend**.

American spelling
The most important differences between British and **American spelling** are:
(1) Most words ending *-our* in British English are spelt *-or* in American English:

GB:	*colour*	*flavour*	*labour*
USA:	*color*	*flavor*	*labor*

Exceptions: *glamour* and *saviour* do not change.

(2) Words ending *-re* in British English are usually written *-er* in American English:

GB:	*theatre*	*centre*	*fibre*
USA:	*theater*	*center*	*fiber*

Exceptions: words ending *-cre* or *-gre* have the same spelling: *acre, massacre, ogre*.

(3) With verbs which may end in *-ise* or *-ize*, British spelling often uses *-ise*, and American always uses *-ize*:

GB:	*specialise*	*realise*	*equalise*
USA:	*specialize*	*realize*	*equalize*

See **-ise/-ize** for more of these verbs.

(4) Most words spelt *-ogue* in British English are spelt *-og* in American English:

GB:	*analogue*	*catalogue*	*dialogue*
USA:	*analog*	*catalog*	*dialog*

(5) In British English some words double their consonants before *-er* or *-ed* and *-ing* (eg those ending in *l* or *p*). This is not the case in American English:

GB:	*equalling*	*kidnapped*	*traveller*
USA:	*equaling*	*kidnaped*	*traveler*

(6) Words derived from Greek and Latin which have *ae* or *oe* in the middle, usually have *e* in American English:

GB:	*encyclopaedia*	*gynaecologist*	*anaesthesia*
USA:	*encyclopedia*	*gynecologist*	*anesthesia*

(7) Other common words which are spelt differently:

GB:	USA:
programme	*program*
bank cheque	*bank check*
defence	*defense*
pretence	*pretense*
speciality	*specialty*

Also see **dates** and **billion**.

among see **between**.

amoral see **immoral**.

an see **a**.

-ance/-ant/-ence/-ent

The correct spelling of words with these endings causes many problems. As there are no clear rules, these lists may be useful:

(1) **-ance/-ant**

acquaintance	*attendance*	*informant*	*participant*
appearance	*constant*	*inhabitant*	*relevance*
assistance	*extravagant*	*maintenance*	*resistance*
assurance	*grievance*	*nuisance*	*vengeance*

(2) **-ence/-ent**

adolescence	consistent	negligence	preference
apparent	convalescence	occurrence	reminiscence
coherent	correspondence	permanent	subsistence
competent	existence	persistent	superintendent

(3) A few words are spelt differently in the noun and adjective forms.

Nouns: *dependant, descendant.*
Adjectives: *dependent, descendent.*

annual/perennial

(1) **annual** means 'yearly':
an annual meeting
my annual salary

It can also mean '(a plant) that lives for one year'.

(2) **perennial** means 'perpetual' or 'recurrent':
a perennial problem
a perennial cold

It can also mean '(a plant) that lives for more than two years'.

-ant   see **-ance**.

ante-/anti-

These prefixes are often confused in written English because the pronunciation is similar.

(1) **ante-** means 'before':
antenatal   ante-bellum

(2) **anti-** means 'against' or 'opposite', and is much more common:
antibiotic   anti-war   anticlockwise   antifreeze

anyway/any way

(1) When written as one word **anyway** means 'at all events' or 'in any case':
He said he would not come but he did, anyway.

(2) When written as two words, the meaning is 'in any manner':
Do it any way you like.

apostrophe

It is important to position **apostrophes** correctly. They are used:

(1) to show possession:

    a) add **'s** to a singular noun: *the girl's book*

       add **'** to a regular plural noun: *the girls' book*

       add **'s** to an irregular plural noun: *the children's book*

       add **'s** to a singular noun ending in -*s*: *Charles's book*

Exception: Biblical, classical, and older names ending in -*s* often have an **apostrophe** only added:

    Guy Fawkes' night   Jesus' birthplace

    b) **Apostrophes** are not used after pronouns or possessive adjectives:

    The book is mine/yours/his/hers/ours/theirs.

    The cat is going to miss its kittens.

Exception: *One* has an **apostrophe**:

    One should deal with one's own problems.

(2) to show the position of the missing letter(s) in a contracted form. Contractions should never be used in formal written English, although they are acceptable in informal writing:

I will	*I'll*	*she has*	*she's*
you are	*you're*	*we cannot*	*we can't*
he had/would	*he'd*	*they will not*	*they won't*

(3) **Apostrophes** are not usual in plural forms:

    cigarettes   lunches   tables   planets

Exception: In the plural form of words which are not usually used in the plural, an **apostrophe** is often used for clarity. *There are too many yes's in this poem.*

Also: In the plurals of single numbers or letters:

    There are three s's in assistant.

    How many 4's are there in 234?

Larger numbers can be written with or without the **apostrophe**:

    the 1990s/the 1990's

    How many 25s/25's are there in 500?

appendix

The plural form can be confusing.

(1) When **appendix** is part of the body, the plural form is **appendixes**.

(2) When **appendix** is 'an addition to a book or document', the traditional plural is **appendices**, but **appendixes** is becoming more widely used, and is also correct.

appreciate

Note the spelling: double *p*.

Also note that **appreciate** must be followed by an object:

I would appreciate it if you could help me.

Not **I would appreciate if you could help me.*

appropriate

Note the spelling: double *p* before a single *p*.

apt/liable/likely/prone

These four adjectives have similar but not identical meanings.

(1) **Apt** means 'tending to':

He is apt to oversleep on Monday mornings.

(2) **Liable** is used in a similar sense, but with the added connotation that the result of the tendency is unpleasant or undesirable:

Drunk drivers are liable to crash.

(3) **Likely** is similar to 'probable':

He is likely to phone this afternoon.

(4) **Prone** is similar to **liable,** but **prone** is often used in the context of suffering from a specific thing:

She is prone to accidents.
She is accident-prone.

argument

This is often misspelt because the verb is spelt with *e*: *argue*. Note that the noun has no *e* after *u*.

as   see **like**.

as ... as

(1) With comparisons, formal English prefers the use of subject pronouns (I, he, she, we, they) after the second **as**:

You are as clever as I.

However, the use of *him/her* is becoming more common than *he/she*, even in a relatively formal style.

In informal English, object pronouns (me, him, her, us, them) are used:

You have got as much chance as us.

(2) When the clause continues with a verb, the subject pronoun must be used:

They are as important as we are.

Not *... as us are.*

(3) There are two possible negative forms: **not as ... as**, and **not so ... as**:

He is not as efficient as she is.
She does not have so much work as he has.

assent/consent

These verbs are close in meaning but they are not synonymous.

(1) To **assent** to something is 'to agree readily, without needing persuasion':

As soon as they had completed their presentation, he assented to their proposals for the project.

(2) To **consent** is 'to agree, but usually after some thought, and possibly retaining some doubts':

After several lengthy meetings, he consented to their proposals.

assistant

Frequently misspelt. Remember: *double s* followed by a single *s*.

assume   see **presume**.

as well   see **also**.

-asy   see **-acy**.

attach   see **detach**.

attempt/intend/propose

These words can be followed by a verb in either the infinitive or the *-ing* form. However, the infinitive is more commom:

> *I attempted to answer the question.*
> *He intended to phone her.*
> *She proposed to postpone the meeting.*

aural/oral

(1) **Aural** means 'pertaining to the ear':
> *It was an aural test, ie a listening test.*

(2) **Oral** means 'relating to the mouth' or 'spoken, not written':
> *It was an oral test, ie a speaking test.*
> *The dentist gave him an oral examination.*

averse/adverse

Often used incorrectly.

(1) **Averse** means 'disinclined to, disapproving, or opposed to.' It is often used in the negative form:
> *I am not averse to women politicians.*
> *They are not averse to drinking beer all night.*

Note: it cannot be used directly before the noun:
> Not **averse weather: *averse politician*

(2) **Adverse** means 'unfavourable, hostile', and is used to describe things more often than people:
> *adverse weather/feedback/reports*

B

bachelor
Note the spelling: no *t*.

backward/backwards   see **forward**.

barely   see **hardly**.

bath/bathe
(1) In British English **bath** is used in the sense of 'to wash the whole body':
Will you bath the baby?

(2) **Bathe** is used to mean 'to apply water to something' and also 'to go swimming':
My feet are very sore, so I am going to bathe them.
It is very hot; shall we go for a bathe?

In American English, **bathe** is used for all senses.

beat   see **win**.

because   see **reason**.

because   see **due to**.

begin/beginner/beginning
Note that the final *n* doubles when a word-ending is added.

begin/commence/start
(1) In written English **begin** is the most common of these words, and is more formal than **start**. **Commence** is more formal than **begin**.

(2) When **begin** or **start** is followed by another verb, it may take either the infinitive or the *-ing* form. The *-ing* form is more usual when referring to 'a long or habitual activity':
I began studying French 15 years ago.
He started to cook/cooking dinner 15 minutes ago.

(3) When **commence** is followed by another verb, it should take the *-ing* form:

The Prime Minister commenced speaking 25 minutes ago.

beside/besides

(1) **Beside** means 'near or next to':

She sat beside the bed.
I live beside the park.

(2) **Besides** means 'in addition':

Do you like other meat, besides pork?
I am too tired to go out, and besides, it is raining.

better

In the phrase 'you'd **better**/he'd **better**' etc, contractions are almost always used in spoken English.

In formal writing, contractions cannot be used and it should be noted that **'d** is short for *had*, not **would*.

The contract had better be signed as soon as possible.

between/among

(1) A common misconception is that **between** should always be used for two objects, and **among** for three or more.

(a) **Between** is used to describe the relationship of one object to two or more separate and distinct objects, which are usually named or numbered:

You can camp between the tree, the river and the wall.
Share out the cake between the three children.
My diary is on the desk, between the newspaper and the dictionary.

(b) **Among** is used in a similar way, but for two or more non-separate or indistinguishable objects, which are not named individually:

You can camp among the trees.
Share out the cake among the children.
My diary is on the desk, among the papers and books.

(2) **Between** is used with *and* not **or*:

The choice is between going to the pub and going to the cinema.

(3) In careful English it is not acceptable to use **between** with **each** or **every** and a singular noun. Although often

seen, this structure is not yet correct in formal English:

He stopped between each song.

Instead, use one of the following structures:

He stopped between songs.
He stopped between one song and the next.
He stopped after each song.

Also see **I/me**.

biannual/biennial

Two words which are frequently confused.

Biannual means 'happening twice a year' and **biennial** means 'happening every two years'.

big/great/large

Big

(1) **Big** refers to size, as does **large**, but **big** is less formal than **large**:

That is a big dinner for such a small child.

(2) **Big** can also refer to 'important events or actions' (as can **great**, which is more formal):

Tomorrow is his big day – he is starting school.

Great

(1) **Great** is normally used with regard to 'important events or actions' or to the quality of something 'outstanding' or 'historically important':

It is a great day for this country.
He was a great president.
It was a great film.

(2) When **great** refers to size, it means 'large and impressive':

There is a great statue in the centre of the square.

Large

This refers to size and to numbers:

a large problem/meeting/group/crowd/number of people/ etc.

billion

A million is 1 000 000 (1 and six zeros) in Britain and the USA. However, a **billion** in Britain is not the same as a **billion** in the USA:

GB: *1 billion = 1 000 000 000 000* (1 and twelve zeros)

USA: *1 billion = 1 000 000 000* (1 and nine zeros)

To confuse the situation further, the US meaning is becoming widespread in Britain, particularly in scientific and economic contexts.

bit

Bit is acceptable in informal English but should be avoided in formal styles. Instead of **bit** or **a bit of**, use the following:

*I would like **a little** peace and quiet.*
*I am not **at all** busy.*
*He has got **a small** problem.*

bi-weekly

Bi-weekly is ambiguous: it can mean 'twice a week', or 'once every two weeks'. To avoid confusion use other terms, such as:

twice weekly/fortnightly/every two weeks/ etc.

The same applies to **bi-monthly**.

blame

Blame is frequently used incorrectly. The correct form is:

He blamed it on me.
Not **He blamed me on it.*

born/borne

In the sense of 'to give birth to' the verb is 'to bear' and the past participle is **borne**:

She has borne five children.

The passive is **born**:

He was born in London.

borrow   see **lend**.

both

(1) A frequent error is to follow **both** by *as well as*. **Both** should be followed by *and*:

She is both tired and cold.
Not **She is both tired as well as cold.*

(2) Ensure that **both** is used with two objects and no more. It is not correct to say:

*She is both tired, cold and hungry.

breath/breathe

The noun is **breath** and the verb is **breathe**:

> *It is so cold that I can see your breath.*
> *I cannot breathe very well in a smoky room.*

bring   see **take**.

bulk

Bulk is used to describe a large mass (an uncountable noun), and not a number:

> *The bulk of our business is done with Germany.*
> *The bulk of the information is stored in the computer.*

When the noun is countable, *most* or *majority* should be used:

> *Most of the students come from Spain.*
> *The majority of the letters are posted in the evening.*

Buddha/Buddhism

Note the spelling: double *d* followed by *h*.

bus

The plural is **buses**, not **busses*.

C

can/may
>In informal English **can** is often used instead of **may** but this is not acceptable in a formal context.
>
>(1) In formal English **can** refers to ability:
>*I can swim. Can you?*
>
>(2) **May** refers to permission:
>*May I swim after breakfast? Yes, you may.*
>Or to probability:
>*I may swim after breakfast; it depends on the weather.*

cannot
>In British English the negative of **can** is written as one word:
>*She cannot attend the meeting.*

canvas/canvass
>**Canvas** is a type of cloth, and to **canvass** is to solicit votes or support.

capital letters
>**Capital letters** are used for:
>
>(1) the important words in the titles of:
>organizations: *the European Commission, the Labour Party, British Rail*
>people: *Dr Purvis, Professor Monroe, President Robinson*
>books, plays, etc: *Romeo and Juliet, Gone with the Wind*
>
>(2) days of the week and the months, (but not the seasons):
>*Tuesday   September*
>
>(3) nationalities:
>*an Irish writer   a Scottish castle   a Mexican meal*
>
>(4) north, south, east and west, but only when they are used as place names:
>*the West End of London   South America   the Far East*

cardinal numbers   see **ordinal numbers**.

Caribbean Sea
Often misspelt. Remember: one *r* and double *b*.

-ce/-se

It can sometimes be difficult to know which of these endings to use. This is not helped by the fact that some words which are pronounced *s* are spelt **-se** while others are spelt **-ce**.
These include:

-ce:		**-se:**	
advance	offence	dense	recompense
commence	pronounce	endorse	response
defence	preference	immense	sense
finance	romance	intense	tense

However, there are some guidelines:
(1) Word endings pronounced *z* are written as **-se**:
    advise   exercise   expertise   revise
For more of these, see **-ise/-ize**.

(2) Words pronounced *s* immediately after a vowel are spelt **-ce**.
These include:

advice	deduce	justice	office
choice	race	price	voice

Exceptions include: *chase, house, mouse, obtuse, profuse, promise*.

(3) Nouns related to adjectives ending in *-ant/-ent* take the **-ce** ending:

different	correspondent	relevant	assistant
difference	correspondence	relevance	assistance

For more of these words, see **-ant/-ent**.

(4) Sometimes a verb and the related noun are spelt differently:
    nouns: *licence   practice*
    verbs: *license   practise*

Note that in American English, both the noun and the verb are written with an *s*: *license/practise*. Also written with an *s* in American English are:
    defence   offence   pretence

-cede/-ceed/-sede

The most common of these endings is **-cede**. The only three words ending in **-ceed** are: *exceed, proceed,* and *succeed.* The only word ending in **-sede** is *supersede.*

censor/censure

To **censor** is to 'delete material from', or to 'forbid publication etc of letters, books, film etc'.

To **censure** is 'to blame', or 'to give an unfavourable opinion':

The government was censured for its handling of the affair.

ceremonial/ceremonious

(1) **Ceremonial** is an adjective which means 'relating to ceremony':

a ceremonial dinner/occasion/etc.

(2) **Ceremonious** is also an adjective, and means 'full of ceremony' with the implication of being 'excessively or inappropriately concerned with ceremony':

I am not impressed by his ceremonious behaviour.

childish/childlike

Both these words mean 'like a child' but **childish** has the added meaning of 'silly', and **childlike** has the added connotation of 'innocent':

Stop that childish behaviour immediately!
She has a certain childlike purity.

classic/classical

(1) The adjective **classic** can mean 'of the highest class or rank', especially in literature or art:

Charles Dickens wrote many classic novels.
Casablanca is a classic film.

(2) **Classic** can also mean 'typical':

This is a classic example of this country's bureaucracy.

(3) **Classical** is an adjective meaning 'pertaining to Greek and Latin studies' or 'to ancient Greece or Rome':

Classical authors are best read in the original.

It also refers to music: 'orchestral and chamber' as opposed to 'jazz, folk music'. Thus, there is a difference between a classic record and a classical one.

collective nouns   see **group**.

colon

A **colon (:)** is often used before:

(1) lists:

I want you to buy me three things: bread, milk, and butter.
The main points are as follows: firstly..., secondly..., and thirdly...

A **dash (–)** could be used with a **colon (:–)** but this is unnecessary.

(2) explanations:

I had to sack him: he was always late for work.
I am not surprised that she failed the exam: she never studied.

(3) quotations:

Paul told me:'I will never forgive her!'
According to Shirley Conran: 'Life is too short to stuff a mushroom.'

comma

There are several areas of confusion where the use of **commas** is concerned:

(1) In lists, **commas** are used to separate items. The last two items, however, need not be separated by a **comma** unless they are long:

She went to Spain, Portugal and Italy for her holidays.
He typed the letters, signed them, and went to the post office to buy stamps.

(2) When giving additional information, **commas** are used to separate this from the rest of the sentence:

Mr James, whose daughter is a lawyer, has decided to emigrate.

(3) **Commas** are used after introductory words:

However, the company survived the recession.
In spite of this, Rita is going to accept the job.

(4) **Commas** can be used before direct speech:

He replied, 'I am not sure what to do.'

commemorate

Note the spelling: double *m* followed by a single *m*.

commence   see **begin**.

committee   see **group**.

compare to/with

(1) **Compare to** means 'to liken or represent a similar':
'Shall I compare thee to a summer's day?'
He compared his fellow committee members to sheep.

(2) **Compare with** is 'to examine, in order to ascertain the extent of similarities or differences':
How does British wine compare with French wine?
Compare his first films with his later ones, to see his development as a director.

Also see **contrast.**

comparisons
  adjectives

When comparing adjectives there are two possible forms, and it can be difficult to know which words take the *-er/-est* form (*small, smaller, smallest*), and which words take *more/most* (*expensive, more expensive, most expensive*). The basic rule is that it depends upon how many syllables there are in the adjective.

(1) adjectives of one syllable:
These end in *-er/-est*:

   old, older, oldest   cheap, cheaper, cheapest

Note that adjectives ending in one consonant, preceded by one vowel, double their final consonant:

   fat, fatter, fattest   big, bigger, biggest

Also note that when the final letter is *y*, it is usually changed to *i*: *dry, drier, driest*

(2) adjectives of two syllables:
   (a) The majority of these take the *more/most* form:
   relaxed, more relaxed, most relaxed
   nervous, more nervous, most nervous

Exceptions: Two-syllable words ending in *y*. These take *-er/-est*: *happy, happier, happiest   easy, easier, easiest*

(b) Some two-syllable words may take either form, but *more/most* is the more usual.

This includes words ending in *-ow, -le,* and *-er*

| narrow | simple | clever |
| hollow | subtle | |

and also includes:

| common | handsome | polite | stupid |
| cruel | pleasant | quiet | tired |

(3) adjectives of three or more syllables:

The majority of these take the *more/most* form:

comfortable, more comfortable, most comfortable

Exceptions: The negatives of two-syllable adjectives ending in *y* take the *-er/-est* ending:

unhappy, unhappier, unhappiest   unfunny, unfunnier, unfunniest

adverbs

The majority of adverbs are formed with *more/most*:

carefully,   more carefully,   most carefully
quietly,   more quietly,   most quietly

Exceptions: Some adverbs are formed with *-er/-est*. The most common are:

| early | hard | long | near |
| fast | late | far | soon |

Also: *often* may take either form but *more/most* is more often used.

comparative/superlative

(1) In general, the comparative is used when comparing two objects or people:

> *I think his first novel is better than his second.*
> *He has lived in London and Paris, and thinks that London is the nicer.*

(2) The superlative form is used when comparing three or more objects or people:

> *It is the best book he has written.*
> *He has lived in several cities and thinks that London is the nicest.*

(3) It is also possible to use the comparative form for a comparison of more than two, if they are not members of the same group:

> *London is nicer than other cities.* (London is not one of the *other* cities.)
> *His novels are more interesting than his plays.* (A novel is not a play.)

complacent/complaisant

Note the different spellings of these words.

(1) **Complacent** means 'self-satisfied':
Take that complacent smile off your face.

(2) **Complaisant** means 'willing to please others':
You should be more assertive, and less complaisant.

complement/compliment

(1) A **complement** is 'that which completes':
A full-bodied red wine is a complement to steak.

(2) A **compliment** is 'an expression of praise or regard':
They complimented their mother on her new dress.

comprehensible/comprehensive

(1) **Comprehensible** means 'capable of being understood':
I need a comprehensible grammar book for a class of ten-year-olds.

(2) **Comprehensive** means 'complete, including everything':
You must write a comprehensive report on the problem, ready for Monday's meeting.

comprise/compose/include

These verbs are similar in meaning, and so are often used incorrectly.

(1) **Comprise** means 'consist of', as in, 'the whole consists of the parts':

> *A football team comprises eleven players.*
> *The committee comprises a doctor, a lawyer and a judge.*

Other structures are not correct in formal English. For example:

> **A football team is comprised of eleven players.*
> **Eleven players comprise a football team.*

(2) **Compose** is similar, but is often used in the passive:

> *A football team is composed of eleven players.*
> *The three people who compose the committee are a doctor, a lawyer and a judge.*

(3) **Include** should not be confused with **comprise**:

> *The committee includes a doctor and a lawyer.* (There are also other committee members.)
> *The committee comprises a doctor and a lawyer.* (They are the only members.)

confidant/confident

Do not confuse the spelling of these words.

(1) A **confidant** is someone who is 'confided in, or entrusted with secrets'.

(2) **Confident** is an adjective meaning 'having full belief, assured':

> *She is confident of passing the exam.*

connoisseur

Easy to misspell. Note the double consonants and the vowel combinations.

conscience/conscious

Note the spelling: *sc* in the middle.

consent   see **assent**.

consequent/subsequent

(1) **Consequent** means 'following as a result':

> *The heavy rain and the consequent flooding made many families homeless.*

(ie the rain caused the flooding.)

(2) **Subsequent** means 'following', but not necessarily as a result:

> *The heavy rain and the subsequent flooding made many families homeless.*

(ie the flooding may not have been caused by the heavy rain, although it occurred after the rain.)

continual/continuous

These words are frequently confused.

(1) **Continual** means 'repeated or frequent':
> *He lost his job because of his continual lateness for work.*

(2) **Continuous** means 'without interruption':
> *I wish that baby would be quiet – he has been crying continuously for over two hours.*

continue

It is not correct to use *on* after **continue**:
> *He continued reading/to read the newspaper.*

Continue may be followed by a verb in the *-ing* or the infinitive form, with little difference in meaning.

continuous see **continual**.

contrast

To **contrast** is 'to examine in order to show difference':
> *He is very clever, in contrast to his brother, who has never passed an exam.*

Also see **compare to/with.**

correspondent/co-respondent

Take care not to confuse these words in written English.

A **correspondent** is 'a person with whom one exchanges letters', while a **co-respondent** is 'a person accused of committing adultery with the respondent in a divorce case'.

council/counsel

Frequently confused in writing because they have the same pronunciation.

(1) A **council** is a committee for 'advice, administration or legislation', and a 'member of a **council**' is known as a **councillor** (especially in local government) or a **council member**:

> *A city council administers a city.*
> *The EC Council of Ministers is the decision-making body of the EC.*

(2) To **counsel** is to 'give advice'. A **counsellor** is 'someone who helps people deal with their personal problems':

> *a marriage guidance counsellor, a debt counsellor, etc.*

Counsel is also the 'legal term for a lawyer in court':

> *The counsel for the defence/prosecution.*

credible/creditable/credulous

(1) **Credible** means 'believable':

> *That is hardly credible! Are you sure that is what happened?*

(2) **Creditable** means 'deserving credit':

> *That is a creditable exam result – I am proud of you.*

(3) **Credulous** means 'too ready to believe':

> *He is so credulous – he believed everything I told him.*

criterion

The plural of this word sometimes causes uncertainty. The singular is **criterion** and the plural is **criteria.**

-ction/-xion

(1) Most words ending in this way are spelt **-ction.** These include:

> *conjunction   extinction   inspection   section*

A few may take either spelling:

> *connection/connexion*   *deflection/deflexion*
> *inflection/inflexion*   *reflection/reflexion*

(2) A few words are spelt **-xion.** The most common are:

> *complexion   crucifixion   genuflexion*

cynic/sceptic

(1) A **cynic** is a person who 'takes a pessimistic view of human nature and actions':

A cynic distrusts politicians, believing them all to be corrupt.

(2) A **sceptic** is a person who 'is doubtful, or who inclines to disbelieve':

A sceptic is not convinced that the government can reduce inflation.

czar/tsar

Both spellings are correct.

D

dash

A **dash** is rarely used in formal writing. In informal writing, it may be used:

(1) to introduce an explanation, instead of a colon or semi-colon.

(2) for an after-thought, instead of brackets.

(3) as well as a colon when introducing a list (:–), but this is unnecessary.

data

Originally **data** was a plural noun, but in modern usage it is also used in the singular:

The data is stored on the computer.

dates

(1) There are several correct ways to write the **date**:

2 September 1992/September 2nd 1992/2nd September 1992

All of these may be written with a comma before the year. The most usual style for a business letter is:

25 October 1993

(2) When in figures, British and American dates are written differently; the month and the day are reversed:

| *1 August 1982* | GB: | *1/8/82* | USA: | *8/1/82* |
| *10 December 1994* | GB: | *10/12/94* | USA: | *12/10/94* |

(3) When using AD or BC note the position:

55BC   AD55

definite/definitive

These words are not synonymous.

(1) **Definite** means 'fixed, clear':

She will give you a definite answer next week.

(2) **Definitive** means 'final, authoritative':

This is the definitive book on European history.

demand

It can be difficult to know which preposition should be used after **demand**.

the verb

(1) When **demand** means 'to require, need', it is followed by *of*:

The computer course demands a lot of its students.

(2) When **demand** means 'to ask for', it is followed by *from*:

He demanded an apology from them.

It may also be followed by the infinitive of a verb:

He demanded to know what had happened.

the noun

(1) When **demand** means 'requirement of effort', it is followed by *on*:

The computer course makes a lot of demands on the students.

(2) When **demand** means 'request, desire', it is followed by *for*:

There is a great demand for this breed of dog.

deny   see **refute**.

depend

In a formal style **depend** must always be followed by *on* or *upon*; the preposition should not be omitted:

He might attend the meeting; it depends upon how busy he is.

dependant/dependent

(1) Note that the noun ends with **-ant**:

How many dependants have you got?

(2) The adjective ends in **-ent**:

He is very dependent upon his mother.

depth   see **height**.

derisive/derisory

(1) **Derisive** means 'mocking':

Their derisive laughter made her cry.

29

(2) **Derisory** means 'so small or unimportant as to be ridiculous':

> *Their derisory pay rise will probably result in industrial action.*

desert/dessert

Note the difference in spelling:

> *the Sahara desert/apple pie for dessert*

detach/attach

Note the spelling: there is no *t* before the *ch*.

diaphragm

Easily misspelt. Note the *gm* at the end.

diarrhoea

Frequently written incorrectly. Note the double *r* followed by *h*, and also the vowel combination at the end.

dice/die

Originally **die** was the singular form and **dice** was the plural, but in modern usage **dice** is used for both singular and plural:

> *Where is/are the dice?*

differ from/to

(1) When **differ** means 'to be unlike', it is followed by *from*:

> *My job differs from yours in several respects.*

(2) When **differ** means 'to disagree', it is followed by *with*:

> *I differ with you on this particular issue.*

different from/to

Both forms are correct, but **different from** is preferred in formal English. **Different than** is not acceptable in formal English.

disinterested see **uninterested.**

distinct/distinctive

Take care not to confuse these words.

(1) **Distinct** means 'separate, different, well-defined':

> *There are three distinct reasons for not going ahead with this.*

(2) **Distinctive** means 'characteristic, distinguishing one person or object from others':

Some actors have very distinctive voices.

distrust   see **mistrust**.

do

Do is often used to avoid repeating a verb:
He asked me to close the door, and I did.

However, there are some common errors in this construction:

(1) In a formal style **do** should not be used to replace *have*:
He has more brothers than I have.
Not **than I do.*
She has travelled more than he has.
Not **more than he has done.*

(2) **Do** should not be used to replace the verb *to be*:
They asked me to be early and so I was.
Not **and so I did.*

Also see **do so**.

do so

In a formal style **do so** can sometimes be used, instead of **do**, to avoid repeating a verb. This is particularly common before adverbs:

He asked me to pick up the broken glass, and I did so very carefully.

I told her I would type it, and I will do so, as soon as I can.

There are several areas where mistakes are often made:

(1) **Do so** should be used with voluntary, deliberate actions, not with involuntary ones.
Compare:

I buy a bar of chocolate every lunchtime and I have always done so.

I like chocolate and I always have done.
Not **have done so.*

(2) **Do so** should be used to refer to the same subject and action as the original verb:

Peter always goes to the cinema on Sundays but I never do.
Not **I never do so.*

31

(3) It is not correct to use **so** after auxiliary verbs other than **do**:

Not **she has so /they can so/I will so/etc.*

downward(s)   see **forward**.

drier/dryer

(1) **Drier** is the comparative form of 'dry':

During the summer Spain is much drier than England.

(2) Both spellings are correct when referring to a machine for drying clothes, hair, etc.

due to

In careful English is is preferable to use **due to** to refer back to a noun, not to a verb:

Their late arrival was due to bad weather.

Not **They arrived late due to bad weather.* (As **due to** here refers to the verb *arrive*.)

* *Due to bad weather they arrived late.* (As **due to** does not refer back to a noun.)

However, the use of **due to** at the beginning of a sentence is becoming increasingly common:

Due to circumstances beyond our control, all trains have been cancelled.

Alternatives to **due to** are:

owing to;   because of;   on account of.

dyeing/dying

(1) **Dyeing** is from the verb 'to dye':

How long have you been dyeing your hair?

(2) **Dying** is from the verb 'to die':

His uncle is dying of cancer.

E

each/every

There are several areas of confusion.

(1) **Each** and **every** are similar but not synonymous.

(a) **Each** is used to emphasize the individuality of the things or people in a group:

Each child in the class has a talent for something.

Each of these books is worth reading.

(b) **Every** is used to emphasize *all* the members of a group:

Every child in the class passed the exam.

Every book in this library may be borrowed.

(2) singular or plural?

(a) When **each** is used before the subject, the singular verb is used:

Each of these children has a pet of some kind.

Each animal is going to be taken to the vet.

(b) When **each** is used after the subject, the plural verb should be used:

The houses each have a different structural fault.

The companies are each holding a Christmas party.

(c) **Every** is used with the singular:

Every cup in the house was dirty.

Every one of these houses is going to be repaired.

each other/one another

Traditionally, **each other** has been used for two people or objects, and **one another** for three or more people or objects. In modern usage this distinction is not strictly applied:

The two children kicked each other/one another.

The four dogs fought with each other/one another.

economic/economical

(1) **Economic** is used when dealing with the field of economics:

The country's economic problems ...; The economic situation...

(2) **Economical** is used to mean 'thrifty or not wasteful':
The smaller car is more economical; it uses less petrol than the larger one.

-ed/-t

Some verbs have two possible endings in the past tense and the past participle. The **-ed** ending is preferred in American English, but in British English the **-t** spelling is preferred:

burn	lean	smell	spill
burnt/burned	leant/leaned	smelt/smelled	spilt/spilled
dream	learn	spell	spoil
dreamt/dreamed	learnt/learned	spelt/spelled	spoilt/spoiled

effect/affect

Two frequently-confused words.

(1) To **effect** is a fairly formal verb meaning 'to accomplish or to bring about something':
The new manager effected great changes.

(2) **Effect** is also a noun meaning 'the result of an action':
The effect of the changes was that many employees lost their jobs.

(3) **Affect** is a verb meaning 'to influence':
These changes affected many employees of the company.

egoist/egotist

The word **egoist** is often used in situations where **egotist** would be more accurate.

(1) An **egoist** is a person who believes in the 'theory of self-interest as the principle of morality', and so acts selfishly because of a philosophical belief.

(2) An **egotist** is a person who 'thinks and speaks too much of himself/herself or of things as they affect himself/herself':
He is such an egotist; he thinks the whole family revolves around him.

ei   see **ie**.

either

Either means 'one thing or the other' and is followed by the third person singular form of the verb:

Either bus goes to the shopping centre.

Either of the companies is capable of delivering the goods.

In informal English, the plural form may be used, particularly in questions and negatives:

Have either of you seen the boss?

I do not think either of them are going to answer the phone.

elder/older

(1) **Older/oldest** can be used to describe relative age in any situation.

(2) **Elder/eldest** are used to describe relative age or seniority within a family or a business:

She is the elder/eldest daughter.

He was the elder/eldest partner.

(3) **Older,** not **elder,** must be used in sentences with *than:*

He is older than his sister.

Not **He is elder than his sister.*

electric/electrical/electronic

(1) **Electric** is used to describe something which produces or is produced by electricity, or which is operated by electricity:

an electric kettle/storm/battery/ etc.

(2) **Electrical** is more general and means 'of or concerned with electricity':

an electrical engineer/an electrical goods department/ etc.

(3) **Electronic** refers to complex electrical apparatus, such as videos, televisions and computers.

elicit/illicit

Take care not to confuse the spellings of these two words.

(1) **Elicit** means 'to draw facts, a response, etc, from somebody, sometimes with difficulty':

The teacher finally elicited an answer from the student.

(2) **Illicit** means 'unlawful' or 'not allowable':
   The police are clamping down on illicit drinking clubs.

embarrass
Easily misspelt. Remember: double *r* and double *s*.

emend/amend
These words are often confused.
(1) To **emend** means 'to remove errors from text, book, etc':
   This agenda must be emended before it is photocopied.

(2) To **amend** is to 'make improvements':
   I am going to amend this report before I show it to my boss.

emigrate   see **immigrate**.

eminent   see **imminent**.

-ence   see **-ance**.

encyclopaedia   see **American spelling**

English
People from England are **English.** People who come from other parts of Great Britain are not **English:** they are *Scottish* or *Welsh*.

-ent   see **-ance**.

enquire/inquire
These both mean 'to ask a question or to make an investigation', but are used in slightly different contexts:
(1) **Enquire** is more often used when desiring general information:
   The tourist enquired about train times to Glasgow.

(2) **Inquire** is used when making a serious study or investigation:
   The police are inquiring into the cause of the murder.

equally

It is not correct to follow **equally** with *as*:

> *His last film was equally good.*
>
> Not **His last film was equally as good.*
>
> Instead, use: *as, equally* or *just as.*

especial(ly)/special(ly)

(1) **Especial(ly)** and **special(ly)** can both be used to mean 'unusual, extreme' or 'particular'. In a formal style, **especial(ly)** is more usual:

> *We must be especially careful that nothing goes wrong.*

(2) When the meaning is 'for a particular purpose', only **special(ly)** is possible:

> *Do I need special insurance to drive abroad?*
>
> *I made this cake specially for you.*

-ess

The use of **-ess** to make nouns feminine is declining. Among the ones still in use are:

actress	*princess* (and other such titles)
air hostess/stewardess	*shop manageress*
lioness	*waitress*

even

In written English, unlike spoken English, it is important to position **even** correctly in order to avoid ambiguity. It should go directly before the word(s) it refers to. Compare:

> *Even the mechanic cleaned the bus.* (Nobody thought *he* would help to clean it.)
>
> *The mechanic even cleaned the bus.* (He did not just repair it; he cleaned it as well.)
>
> *The mechanic cleaned even the bus.* (As well as cleaning other things.)

ever

A common area of confusion is when words such as **whatever** should be written as one word, or as two: **what ever**.

(1) When **ever** is used after interrogative words such as *what, who, where*, it adds emphasis and is written as two words:

What ever are you wearing?
How ever did you get here so quickly?

(2) When **ever** is added to interrogative words to form one word, the meaning is 'no matter what', 'no matter when' etc:

Whenever you phone, we will be at home.
However you look at it, we have a problem.

(a) **Whatever** also means 'anything that':
Children should do whatever their parents tell them.

(b) **Whenever** can also be used to mean 'each time when':
Whenever I see him, he looks younger.

(c) **Whoever** also means 'anybody who' or 'the person who':
Whoever did this must be really stupid.

every see **each**.

everyday/every day

(1) **Everyday** is an adjective meaning 'daily' or 'usual' and goes before a noun:
This is an everyday occurrence.

(2) **Every day** consists of an adjective, **every**, describing a noun, **day**:
I go to work every day.

everyone/every one
Note the difference.
(1) **Everyone** is the same as 'everybody', and is used for groups of people:
Everyone I know prefers cats to dogs.

(2) **Every one** may be used for people or, more often, for things, and means 'each individual one':
She bought four books and read every one twice.
Also see **each/every**.

exaggerate

Note the spelling: only the *g* is doubled.

except

In very formal English, **except** should be followed by subject pronouns (I, he, she, we, they). Less formal styles use object pronouns (me, him, her, us, them):

Everyone arrived on time except he/him.

Nobody enjoyed the conference except I/me.

extensive   see **intense**.

F

fairly/quite/rather
These words are used to express different degrees of intensity.
  (1) **Fairly** is the weakest:
      It is fairly cold out; wear a jacket.

  (2) **Quite** is stronger than **fairly**:
      It is quite cold out; wear a coat.

  (3) **Rather** is the strongest of these:
      It is rather cold out; wear a warm coat.

family   see **group**.

farther/further
  (1) Both **farther** and **further** are used to describe physical distance:
      How much farther/further is the beach?

  (2) **Further** also means 'in addition' and 'to a greater degree':
      Further education/further news reports/ etc.

February
A frequently misspelt word: note the *r* in the middle.

feet/foot   see **weights and measures**.

few/a few
These are both used to refer to plural, or countable, nouns: *people, cars, apples, bottles of milk, etc.*
(1) **Few** has a negative sense and is used to mean 'not many':
      The teacher had never taught history before, and few students passed the exam.

(2) **A few** has a more positive meaning and is closer to 'some':
      The exam was extremely difficult but a few students passed.
Also see **little/a little** and **fewer/less**.

fewer/less

These are often used incorrectly.

(1) **Fewer** is used for plural nouns (things which can be counted; countables):

cars	cigarettes	meetings	problems
cans of orange	complaints	people	terrorists

(2) **Less** is used for singular or mass nouns (uncountables):

heat	orange juice	sugar	time
money	smoke	terrorism	traffic

fight with

To **fight with** somebody can mean both 'to fight on the same side' and 'to fight on the opposite side':

The Americans fought with the British, against the Germans, in World War II.

The Americans fought with the Germans in World War II.

Make sure your meaning is clear from the context.

first/firstly

When making a list, all these forms are correct:

First..., second..., third...
First..., secondly..., thirdly...
Firstly..., secondly..., thirdly...

flammable/inflammable

These words are frequently used incorrectly as **inflammable** is thought of as a negative adjective. Both **flammable** and **inflammable** mean 'able or likely to burn'. To form the negative, *non-* is added:

non-flammable/non-inflammable

foot   see **weights and measures**.

fore-/for-

(1) **Fore-** is added to the front of words to give the meaning 'before, beforehand, in front':

to forecast   foreground   foreword (of a book)
forefather   foregone (conclusion)

(2) Words beginning **for-** are less common. They include:

forbid   forget   forlorn   forward (direction)
forfeit   forgive   forsake

former/latter

Former refers to the first in a list of two things; **latter** refers to the second and last:

Both Kathy and Simon failed the exam; the former because she had not studied, and the latter because he did not take it.

For a good clear style, they are better avoided.

forward/forwards

(1) Both **forward** and **forwards** can be used as adverbs:
She stepped forward(s) to greet her guests.
He drove forward(s) to make space for the other car.

Exception: In the case of *look forward to* only **forward** is correct.
Forward is becoming more usual than **forwards.**

(2) As an adjective, only **forward** is correct:
a forward movement/the forward part of a ship

(3) The same applies to other words ending in *-ward(s)*:
backward(s)   homeward(s)   upward(s)

-ful

(1) When **-ful** is added to words to form adjectives, take care not to add double *l*:
careful   helpful

(2) The plural of nouns ending in **-ful** is formed by adding *s* to the end:
3 cupfuls   (not **cupsful*)   *2 spoonfuls* (not **spoonsful*)

full stop   see **abbreviations**.

further   see **farther**.

G

gas
The plural of the noun has one *s*: **gases**.

gaol/jail
Both forms are correct in British English, but **jail** is becoming more usual. In American English, only **jail** is used.
Be careful not to confuse *goal* with **gaol**.

get/got
(1) In formal written English it is better to use *have* instead of the more informal *have got*:
> *He had to reimburse me.*
> *I did not have an appointment at eleven o'clock.*

(2) In written English **get/got** should be avoided; instead, use a verb with a more specific meaning, such as:
> *arrive, buy, receive, obtain.*

ghastly/ghetto/ghost
Note the spelling of these words: the *h* comes directly after the *g*.

gipsy/gypsy
Both forms are correct, but **gypsy** is more usual.

gonorrhoea
Easily misspelt. In American English it is spelt **gonorrhea**.

gorilla   see **guerilla**.

got   see **get**.

government   see **groups**.

groups
A common problem area is whether words such as *committee*, *family* and *group* are singular or plural. These

words are known as collective nouns, and may be either singular or plural, depending on the context.

(1) When the group is viewed as a single unit, the singular form of the verb is used:

> *The committee is going to meet every Monday.*
> *The Samson family is in London.*
> *The pop group is making a record.*

(2) When the group is viewed as a collection of individuals, the plural form of the verb is used:

> *The committee have been arguing all morning.*
> *The Samson family are all musicians.*
> *The pop group are very good-looking.*

(3) In formal English it is not acceptable to change from singular to plural, or vice versa, within the same sentence, regardless of point of view:

Incorrect: **The committee is pleased to announce their decision.*
Correct: *is ... its/are ... their*

(4) Other collective nouns include:

audience	company	headquarters	public
the BBC	crew	jury	school
choir	crowd	majority	staff
class	firm	orchestra	team
club	government	police	union

guarantee

Note the the *u* comes directly after the *g*.

guerilla/guerrilla/gorilla

Both **guerilla** and **guerrilla** are correct spellings, although the double *r* form is more common.

Neither of these should be confused with **gorilla**, which is a type of African ape.

gynaecologist

Note the spelling. See also **American spelling**.

gypsy   see **gipsy**.

H

haemorrhage

This is easily misspelt. All such words concerned with blood begin **haem**: *haemophiliac, haemorroid.*

In American English they begin **hem**: *hemorrhage.*

half (of)

(1) When **half** is used with a singular noun it takes a singular verb:

Half the trouble is the weather.
Half the film was in French.

(2) When the noun is plural, the verb is too:

Half the workers are on holiday today.
Half the boys are playing tennis.

(3) **Half of**

Before a noun the **of** is optional:

Half (of) the buses will be late.

However, it is necessary before a pronoun:

Half of them will be late.

Exception: With times or quantities *of* is not used:

half a dozen   half a kilo   half an hour

hang/hanged/hung

Hang has two meanings, with different past tenses and past participles.

(1) **Hang, hung, hung**:

She hung the Christmas decorations on the tree.
Have you hung their coats up?

(2) **Hang, hanged, hanged,** meaning 'to put to death by suspending by the neck':

The murderer was hanged at 6am.

hanger/hangar

Take care not to confuse these spellings:

Clothes are kept on hangers, and planes are kept in hangars.

harass

Often misspelt. Note: one *r* and double *s*.

hardly/barely/scarcely

These words are followed by *when* or *before*, not **than*:

The match had hardly started before it began to rain.

I had barely got into the bath when the phone rang.

he/she see **they**.

height/depth

Height is the 'measure of distance upwards':

a mountain or a building.

Depth is the 'measure of distance down or inwards':

a river, a hole, a cave.

help

In a formal style **help** is usually followed by an object (*me, him, Joanne, etc*) and *to*:

Would you mind helping me to complete this form?

hiccup/hiccough

Although both spellings are acceptable, **hiccup** is preferred.

high see **tall**.

hire/let/rent

These words all have the same basic meaning: 'to buy or sell the use of something'. However, they are used in different contexts.

(1) **Hire** is used when referring to a short period of time:

You hire a car, a boat, a tuxedo, a room for a party, etc.

(2) **Rent** is used with longer periods of time:

You rent a flat, a house, a TV, a video player, etc. (It may also be used for a car.)

(3) **Let** is also used for longer periods of time, but only for property, and only in the sense of selling the use of the property. We often see signs: *house to let, offices to let, etc.*

historic/historical

There is often uncertainty about which of these to use.

(1) **Historic** means 'famous or important in history':

a historic building/city/battle/ etc.

(2) **Historical** means 'concerned with history' or 'having an actual existence in history':

a historical novel/society/play/ etc.
Many people believe that Sherlock Holmes was a historical character.

hors d'œuvre(s)

Notice the spelling. The *s* in the plural form is optional.

however

When **however** is used to contrast one statement with another, it should be separated from the rest of the sentence by commas:

However, that can be decided tomorrow.
The students, however, did not want to have an exam.

For the difference between **however** and **how ever** see **ever**.

hung see **hang**.

hyphen

It can be difficult to know where a **hyphen** should be used. For queries about specific words, consult a good dictionary.

Here are some general guidelines which may be of some help:

(1) In general, a **hyphen** is used to show that two or more words should be viewed as one:

blue-eyed	*ex-husband*	*heart-breaking*	*make-up*
mother-in-law	*non-stick*	*out-of-work*	*self-sown*

(2) A **hyphen** should be used when a prefix is added to a word beginning with a capital letter:

ex-Christian   un-English   anti-Europe

(3) In order to avoid ambiguity, a **hyphen** can be used to link words:

a Scottish whisky-producer (the producer is Scottish)
a Scottish-whisky producer (the whisky is Scottish)

Also: to avoid ambiguity where words are similar:

How did your mother react to the news?
They are going to re-act the last scene of the play.

They would like to reform the electoral system.
Do you think that pop group will re-form?

(4) A **hyphen** is sometimes used to avoid joining two *e*'s, or two of the same consonants:

re-establish   re-educate   heart-throb

(5) Numbers from twenty-one to ninety-nine have **hyphens**, as do fractions: *one-third, three-quarters, etc.*

(6) When a word needs to be divided, owing to lack of space at the end of a line, a **hyphen** is used.
Position the **hyphen** to give an idea of the whole word, and also of the pronunciation:

for-get not **fo-rget*
negotia-tions not **negotiat-ions*
musi-cian not **music-ian*

I

I/me

When to use **I** or **me** causes a great deal of confusion.

(1) After prepositions **I** is often used in the mistaken belief that it is better grammar. **Me,** not **I,** should be used after prepositions. This error is particularly common when two or more people follow the preposition:

The children will come with Ann and me. Not **... Ann and I.*
She sat between Susan and me. Not **... Susan and I.*
He wrote to you and me Not **... you and I.*

(2) After the verb *to be,* **me** is correct, not **I**. In modern usage **I** seems over-formal:

It is me. Not **It is I.*

However, in formal English **I** is correct when there is a following clause:

It was I who wrote the letter.
It is I who shall be signing the contract.

(3) The above rules apply for all persons:

I/me, he/him, she/her, we/us, they/them.

For the use of **I/me** with comparisons see **than**.

-ible   see **-able**.

-ic/-ical   see individual entries.

ei/ie

This is a common spelling problem.

(1) The rule is 'i before e except after c':

ceiling   conceive   receive

However, the vowels must come directly after *c* or this does not apply:

chandelier   chief

(2) If the vowels rhyme with *say* or *air*, spell them **ei**:

beige   eight   heir   weight

(3) Among the exceptions are:

ie

ancient	*deficient*	*proficient*	*sufficient*
conscience	*efficient*	*species*	

ei

caffeine	*forfeit*	*leisure*	*seize*
either	*heifer*	*neither*	*sovereign*
foreign	*height*	*protein*	*weird*

if

(1) A frequent error in sentences containing **if** is to use an extra *have* or *of*. This is particularly common when contractions are used, but is never acceptable:

If he had done it, I would have paid him.

Not **If he had have done it, I would have paid him.*

If she had seen you, she would have said hello.

Not **If she had of seen you, she would have said hello.*

(2) It can be difficult to know whether to use **was** or **were** in conditional sentences.

(a) When the situation is a purely hypothetical one, use **were**:

If I were you I would take an aspirin.

If she were an animal, she would be a cat.

(b) When the situation is a likely or possible one, use **was**:

If that was my bus, I shall be late for work.

If she was here, she could fix it.

(3) In formal English, **whether** is preferred to **if** in indirect questions:

Can you tell me whether the solicitor handles divorce cases?

Do you know whether the play begins at 7.30 or at 8?

illegible/unreadable

These words are not synonymous.

(1) **Illegible** refers to the quality of handwriting or print, and means 'unclear' or 'not capable of being read':

This essay is illegible. You must improve your handwriting.

(2) **Unreadable** refers to the content of a piece of writing, and means 'not capable of being read with pleasure or interest':

This book is unreadable; it put me to sleep.

illicit   see **elicit**.

illusion   see **allusion**.

immigrate/emigrate

(1) To **immigrate** is 'to enter a country in order to live there'. A person who does this is an **immigrant:**

There are many Irish immigrants in the USA.

(2) To **emigrate** is 'to leave your own country in order to settle in another one'. A person who **emigrates** is an **emigrant**:

Many Irish people have emigrated to the USA.

imminent/eminent

(1) **Imminent** means 'impending, about to happen' and is usually used in a negative context:

imminent job losses/trouble/bus strike/ etc.

(2) **Eminent** means 'conspicuous, distinguished':

an eminent lawyer/surgeon/ etc.

immoral/amoral

Take care not to confuse these words.

(1) **Immoral** means 'not following accepted moral principles':

Films thought to be immoral are often banned.

(2) **Amoral** means 'having no understanding of right or wrong':

In his opinion, children and animals are completely amoral.

imply/infer

In modern usage, **imply** is often used as a synonym of **infer**. This is not acceptable in formal English.

(1) To **imply** means 'to express (something) indirectly, to insinuate':

Are you implying that my son is stupid?
The reference implied that he was an unsatisfactory employee.

(2) To **infer** means 'to draw a conclusion from a statement':

> *Am I to infer, from this school report, that my son is stupid?*
> *I inferred from the reference that he was an unsatisfactory employee.*

in-/un-

When forming a negative it can be difficult to know whether to use **in-** or **un-**. There are no clear rules, but these guidelines may be of some help:

(1) Words with the following endings take **in-**:

-ible	*inflexible*
-uble	*insoluble*
-ence/-ent	*independent*
-ity	*inequality*
-ice	*injustice*
-tude	*ingratitude*

Exceptions:

Words beginning with *l* take *il-*: *illegible*
Words beginning with *r* take *ir-*: *irresponsible*
Words beginning with *b*, *p* or *m* take *im-*:

> *imperceptible   immaturity*

(2) **Un-** is used in words which end:

-ed	*uneducated*	*unmodernised*
-ing	*unbelieving*	*untiring*

Common exceptions:

> *incapacitated   indisposed   inexperienced*

include   see **compose**.

independent

Note the spelling: all the vowels, except the first one, are *e*'s.

index

This word has two plural forms: **indexes** is used in the context of books and papers, and **indices** is used in the context of science and mathematics.

infer   see **imply**.

inferior

In comparisons, **inferior** should be followed by *to*, not *than*:

> *Is Bulgarian wine inferior to German?*

inflammable   see **flammable**.

inflict/afflict

(1) To **inflict** is to 'impose (something or someone unpleasant or unwanted) on or upon someone':

> *He inflicted his horrible children on us for the afternoon.*

(2) **Afflict** means 'to cause to suffer in the body or mind; to trouble'. It is often used in the passive followed by *with* or *by*:

> *He is afflicted with hayfever.*
> *The major problem afflicting the present government is ...*

ingenious/ingenuous

Take care with the final vowel combinations.

(1) **Ingenious** means 'clever at finding imaginative solutions to problems':

> *What an ingenious idea! How did you think of it?*

(2) **Ingenuous** means 'open, frank, innocent':

> *She is such an ingenuous girl. I do not think she should go abroad alone.*

inquire   see **enquire**.

intend   see **attempt**.

intense/intensive/extensive

(1) **Intense** is an adjective which means 'strong or great' or 'having some quality in a high degree':

> *intense pain/hatred/competition/ etc.*

(2) **Intensive** is an adjective which means 'employing much effort, concentrated':

> *intensive efforts/course of study/care* (in hospital)/ *etc.*

(3) **Extensive** is an adjective which means 'large, far-reaching, comprehensive':

> *As a result of the crash, extensive repairs must be carried out.*

inverted commas   see **quotation marks**

-ise/-ize

In British English many verbs may take either the **-ise** or the **-ize** ending. Some *must* take the **s** spelling. Therefore, if in doubt, use the **-ise** form.

Common verbs which may take either **s** or **z**:

*antagonise/ize   fertilise/ize   nationalise/ize   publicise/ize
baptise/ize   finalise/ize   maximise/ize   recognise/ize
criticise/ize   itemise/ize   privatise/ize   sympathise/ize*

In American English the **z** spelling of these words is preferred.

Note: *capsize, prize,* and *size* must always be spelt **-ize.**

its/it's

These are often confused in written English because the pronunciation is the same.

(1) **Its** is the possessive form of *it* and there is no apostrophe:

*The dog likes its kennel.
Our theatre is going to lose its funding.*

(2) **It's** is the contracted form of *it is* and *it has,* and is only used in an informal context:

*It's a difficult subject.
It's rained a lot recently.*

-ize   see **-ise**.

J

jail   see **gaol**.

jewellery/jewelry

Both spellings are correct, but **jewellery** is more common in British English and **jewelry** in American English.

join

In written English, following **join** with *together* is not desirable:

These departments are going to be joined in the near future.
Not * *... joined together in the near future.*

judgement/judgment

Both of these spellings are correct. The first is more common in British English.

junction/juncture

These words are often confused.

(1) A **junction** is 'a place where two things join or come together':

a railway junction/a road junction/ etc.

(2) A **juncture** is 'a particular point in time or in a course of events':

At this critical juncture in negotiations...

K

kind of

A common problem is whether **kind of** should be used with the singular or the plural. Modern usage recommends.

This kind of book is ...
Books of this kind are ...

The same applies to **sort of**.

knit

(1) When **knit** is used to refer to knitting items of clothing, the past tense and past participle are usually **knitted**:

I knitted her a scarf.

(2) In other senses, the past tense and past participle are usually **knit**:

He knit his brows.
The bone should knit in a few weeks.

L

lack/absence

(1) **Lack** means 'the state of not having (enough of) something':

> *Lack of money prevented him from going home for Christmas.*

(2) **Absence** means 'non-presence, non-existence':

> *The absence of accurate information makes our job very difficult.*

large   see **big**.

latter   see **former**.

lay/lie

Frequently confused words, particularly in the past tense.

(1) **Lay, laid, laid**:

To **lay** is to 'put down carefully' or 'put down flat'. It normally takes a direct object (you **lay** *something*):

> *Have you laid the papers on the table?*
> *Lay the wedding dress on the bed.*

(2) **Lie, lay, lain**:

To **lie** means 'to be down, to be flat'. A direct object is not necessary, but if there is one, it is usually animate:

> *Lie the baby on the bed.*
> *How long has he lain there like that?*
> *I lay on the beach all morning.*

lend/loan/borrow

(1) **Lend** is always a verb. The meaning is similar to 'give':

> *Can you lend me £10?*
> *I lent you £15 yesterday.*

(2) **Loan** has the same meaning but can be used as a noun and, less often, as a verb:

> *This bank gives loans to students.*

(3) **Borrow** is always a verb. The meaning is similar to 'take':

> *Can I borrow £10* (from you)?
> *You borrowed £15* (from me) *yesterday.*

lengthy/long

These words are similar but not synonymous. **Lengthy** is used to mean 'long and tedious', and is usually applied to speech or writing:

> *a lengthy speech/meeting/document/ etc.*

less see **fewer**.

let see **hire**.

letter writing

There are several areas to note:

(1) Style

In formal writing, such as business letters, a formal style is necessary. However, this does not mean that stilted language with long complex sentences should be used.
Remember that the purpose of writing is communication and aim for a clear, easy-to-read style.

(2) Punctuation

The present trend in writing is to reduce the number of commas, full stops, etc to create an 'uncluttered' appearance. Therefore, addresses and dates etc may be written without punctuation.
In a formal style, contractions of verbs (*I'll, you'd*, etc) are not acceptable.
Also see **abbreviations**.

(3) Beginnings and endings

Letters should have an ending which is appropriate to their beginning. A comma may be used after the salutation or the ending, but is now often omitted.

    (a)   If you do not know the name of the person to whom you are writing,

> begin: *Dear Sir   Dear Madam   Dear Sir/Madam*
> end: *Yours faithfully*

    (b)   If you know the name of the person to whom you are writing,

begin:	*Dear Mr ...*
	Dear Ms ...
end:	*Yours sincerely*

More informal endings are: *Yours*   *Best Wishes*

For more details on how to address women, see **Miss**.

(4) Layout

There are several possible variations in style, but formal letters in modern English are usually arranged on the page like this:

---

17 Sword Rd
London
W21 4RJ

15 September 1992

Holiday Cottages
25 Holme St
Oxford
OX19 2RE

Dear Sir/Madam

I saw your advertisement for holiday cottages, in yesterday's *Guardian*.

Could you please send me a copy of your brochure and include details of Christmas breaks?

I look forward to hearing from you.

Yours faithfully

John Smith

Points to note:
(a) The address is written in a 'block' style, without punctuation. However, commas can be used at the end of each line, and full stops can be used for abbreviations.

(b) In this case, the date is written without punctuation. For more details, see **dates**.

(c) In a formal letter, the name and address of the person to whom you are writing should be put on the left side.

(d) A 'block' style is used throughout: each line begins at the left margin and new paragraphs are shown by leaving a line blank.

An alternative style, more common in handwriting, is to indent each new paragraph (beginning approximately 2cm from the left margin).

(e) A new paragraph should be started for each change of subject.

liable   see **apt**.

libel/slander

These are frequently used incorrectly.

(1) **Libel** is 'any false or malicious defamatory publication or statement'. This includes writing, print, broadcasting and pictures.

(2) **Slander** is similar, but applies to spoken words (not broadcast), looks, signs, and gestures.

licence/license

The noun is spelt **licence** but the verb is spelt with an **-se** ending.

lie   see **lay**.

lighted/lit

As the past tense and past participle of the verb *light*, both these forms are correct: **light**, **lighted**, **lit**; and **light**, **lit**, **lit**. In British English **lit** is more common.

As an adjective, however, **lighted** is more common.

lightening/lightning

(1) When this word is written with an *e*, it is the present participle and gerund of the verb '**to lighten**':

The sky is lightening; the sun must be rising.
The government is lightening the burden of taxation.
It has been thundering and lightening for the last two hours.

(2) Without an *e*, this word is a noun:
a flash of lightning/a lightning conductor/ etc.
Also in other senses:
a lightning strike/decision/ etc.

like/as

(1) In formal English **like** is not acceptable as a conjunction (ie followed by a subject and a verb). Instead, use **as,** or *as if/as though*:
Have you done it as I told you to?
Not **Have you done it like I told you to?*
It looks as if she is going to be promoted.
Not **It looks like she is going to be promoted.*

In sentences where the verb is understood, but not stated, **like** may be used with a noun:
She sounds as if she is an American/She sounds like an American.

(2) To say how something really is, or was, use **as** and a noun:
He works as a gardener.
Originally, our house was used as a hotel.

For a hypothetical or unreal situation, **like** and a noun is used:
He drinks like a fish.
We have so many guests that our house is like a hotel.

like doing/to do

(1) When **to like** means 'to enjoy' it can be followed by a noun, or a verb in either the *-ing* or infinitive form:
I like going/to go to the beach.

(2) When **to like** means 'to choose' or 'to be in the habit of', it is followed by a verb in the infinitive form:
I like to have a snack at lunchtime, and then a big meal in the evening.

like/unlike

In comparisons using **like** or **unlike,** object pronouns (me, him, her, us, them) are used:
Like my sister and me, Jonathan is trying to give up smoking.
Not **Like my sister and I ...*

likely see **apt**.

lit see **lighted**.

literally

In formal English it is preferable to use **literally** only in the sense of 'exactly as stated', 'really':

The library has literally thousands of books.

It should not be used to give emphasis:

*There were literally millions of people at the party.

little/a little

Little and **a little** are both used with uncountable, or mass, nouns: **rice**, **sugar**, **smoke**, **wine**, **tea**, etc.

(1) **Little** is used to mean 'not much':

There is little wine left. I will open another bottle.

(2) **A little** is similar to 'some':

There is a little wine left. Who would like some more?

little see **small**.

loan see **lend**.

long see **lengthy**.

loose/lose

(1) **Loose** is the opposite of 'tight', 'exact':

a loose jacket/agreement/ etc.

(2) **Lose** is the verb meaning 'to no longer have something'.

lot

In formal writing, **a lot of** and **lots of** should be avoided, for reasons of style. Instead, use: *a great deal; a great many;* or specific numbers: *several hundred, etc.*

M

mathematics   see **statistics**.

may   see **can**.

maybe/may be
   (1) **Maybe** means 'perhaps':
      Maybe he will phone later.
   In formal English, 'perhaps' is preferred.

   (2) **May be** consists of one verb **may** followed by another verb **be**:
      He may be late.

me   see **I**.

me/my
   When the *-ing* form of the verb is preceded by a pronoun, the possessive form should be used (my, his, her, its, your, our, their):
      I hope you do not mind my leaving early.
      Not *... me leaving early.*
      I am pleased at his being promoted.
      Not *... at him being promoted.*
      Is there any chance of its breaking down again?
      Not *... of it breaking down again?*

media
   The **media** (ie newspapers, television and radio) is often used as a singular noun, but this is not correct. **Media** should be followed by the plural form of verbs:
      The media are opposed to censorship.

mediaeval/medieval
   Both spellings are correct, with **medieval** now being more widely used.

Mediterranean Sea
   Note the spelling: double *r* in the middle, with *ea* later.

meet/meet with

In British English, one **meets** a person, but **meets with** approval, an accident, opposition, etc. **Meet with** a person is correct in American English.

Miss/Mrs/Ms

Mrs, Miss and **Ms** all refer to the marital status of women. **Ms** is frequently used, particularly in letters, when the writer does not know the marital status of the woman addressed. However, the use of **Ms** to avoid distinction is becoming increasingly common even when the marital status of the woman is known to the writer.

In spoken English, **Ms** is rarely used in Britain, although it may be heard in the USA.

mistrust/distrust

These words are similar, meaning 'lack of trust'. However, **distrust** is the stronger, suggesting a 'greater doubt, suspicion or lack of trust' than **mistrust.**

mortgage

Note the spelling: *t* in the middle.

Moslem/Muslim

Both these forms are correct, but **Muslim** is now more common.

Mrs/Ms   see **Miss**.

Muslim   see **Moslem**.

my   see **me**.

N

narcissism

Often spelt incorrectly: note the *c* and double *s*.

naught see **nought**.

near/near to

(1) In the context of physical distance, **near** can be used without **to**. However, the comparative and superlative are normally used with **to**:

> *He works near the bus station.*
> *She lives the nearest to the sports centre.*

(2) **Near to** is normally used when not referring to physical distance:

> *During the wedding, she was near to tears.*
> *He was very near to losing his temper with the children.*

necessary

Frequently misspelt. Remember: one *c* followed by double *s*.

negatives

Two **negatives** are often used together to give a **negative** meaning, but this is not correct.

In English, two **negatives** together cancel out each other and create an affirmative.

Compare:

> *Do nothing.* (ie Be still, do not do a thing.)
> *Do not do nothing.* (ie Do something.)

Two **negatives** may be used, to give an affirmative meaning:

> *I cannot not go.* (ie I must go.)
> *I would not be surprised if he did not come.* (ie I would be surprised if he came.)

However, in a formal style, this should be avoided.

Also: take care when using words such as *barely, hardly, scarcely,* and *without,* which are negative in meaning but not in form:

He can hardly read.
Not **He cannot hardly read.*

neither

Neither is used when referring to two things, and, in formal English, the verb which follows should be singular:

Neither exhibition is interesting.
Neither of her brothers likes football.

When referring to more than two, use **none**.

Neither ... nor

(1) When joining two negatives, use **neither** with **nor**, not * *or*:

Neither he nor his sister smokes.

(2) The verb may take either a singular or plural form, but should agree with the noun or pronoun nearest to it:

Neither Debra nor I am married.
Not **... are married.*
Neither John nor his children want a computer.
Not* *... wants a computer.*

Exception:
If the first noun is plural, the verb should also be plural:

Neither the children nor John want a computer.
Not **... wants a computer.*

(3) It is important to ensure that **neither** is positioned correctly. It should go next to the construction it introduces:

He plays neither tennis nor golf.
Not **He neither plays tennis nor golf.*

nice

This word is over-used. If possible, choose a more descriptive adjective.

none too

In formal English **none too** is preferable to *not too*:

He was none too impressed by their behaviour.

no-one/no one

(1) **No-one** and **no one** both mean 'nobody'.
(2) **No one** can also mean 'no single person':

No one of them could have done all that damage.
No one person is at fault.

not only ... but also

In written English, it is important to ensure that these words are positioned correctly, to **balance** the sentence. This is no problem when **not only** refers to a verb:

She not only takes photographs but also prints them herself.

When **not only** refers to a noun, it should go directly before that noun:

He works not only as a postman but also as a musician.
Not *He not only works as a postman but also as a musician.*

noticeable

Note the spelling: the *e* of *notice* is not dropped when *able* is added.

nought/naught

These words are normally used in different contexts. **Nought** is used for the number, zero, and **naught** is used in expressions such as 'set at naught'.

O

O   see **oh**.

obscene
   Note the spelling: *sc* in the middle.

occasional
   Frequently misspelt. Note the double *c* and the single *s*.

offence/offensive
   Note that the noun is spelt with a *c*, but that the adjective
   has an *s*

oh/O
   (1) **Oh** is the usual form in modern English, and is
   followed by a comma or exclamation mark:
      Oh, I am not sure about that.
      Oh dear! I have broken my watch.

   (2) **O** is rarely used, but may be found in literary or
   religious contexts.

older   see **elder**.

on account of   see **due to**.

one
   (1) **One** can be used to talk about people in general. The
   verb takes the third person singular form:
      One has to carry an identity card in many European countries.
      Which side of the road does one drive on in Japan?

   You may also be used, but is more informal than **one**.
   Ensure that the use of **one** is consistent: do not change to
   he/you etc in mid-sentence:
      One must put one's family first.
      Not *One must put his family first.*

   However, this change is acceptable in American English.

   (2) The use of **one** as a more formal way of saying **I** is
   declining and is best avoided, even in a formal style.

(3) Ensure that the subject and verb agree, ie that both are singular:

One in every four people watches videos. (ie one...watches..)

or that both are plural:

I am one of those people who watch the news six times a day. (ie people...watch...)

(4) Note that as a possessive adjective, **one** has an apostrophe:

Eating a lot of chocolate is bad for one's teeth.

one another   see **each other**.

only

It is important to position **only** correctly. To avoid ambiguity, **only** should go directly before the word or phrase it refers to:

Compare:

Only Mike played the guitar. (Nobody but Mike played it.)

Mike only played the guitar. (He did not do anything else with it.)

Mike played only the guitar. (He did not play any other instrument.)

oral   see **aural**.

ordinal/cardinal numbers

Ordinal numbers are: *first, second, third, etc.*

Cardinal numbers are: *one, two, three, etc.*

orthopaedic

Note the spelling: *ae* in the middle, in British English. See also **American spelling**.

owing to   see **due to**.

P

paragraphs

A common error in writing is to forget to begin a new **paragraph** for each change of subject. Long **paragraphs**, containing several subjects, can be very difficult for the reader to follow.

A new **paragraph** can be shown by leaving a line blank, as in this entry. An alternative style, more common in handwriting, is to indent each new **paragraph** (ie beginning approximately 2cm from the left-hand margin).

parallel

Easily misspelt: only one *r*, with double *l* in the middle.

part from/with

(1) **Part from** means 'to leave, separate':

She parted from her father on bad terms.

(2) **Part with** means 'to give up, give away':

He found it difficult to part with money.

passed/past

These are often confused in written English because the pronunciation is the same.

(1) **Passed** is the past tense and past participle of the verb *to pass*:

Has he passed his driving test yet?

I passed Sylvia in the street yesterday.

(2) **Past** is the form used in all other senses:

I drove past the school.

We can learn a great deal from the past.

He has lived there for the past three years.

people/persons

The usual plural of **person** is **people**. However, **persons** may be used in a formal, official, or technical sense:

Persons without an appointment should go to the reception area.

She was attacked by a person or persons unknown.

per

In written English **per** is used, rather than *a/an*:
  He earns £100 per day.
  They were driving at 90 miles per hour.

perennial   see **annual**.

persons   see **people**.

plural   see **singular**.

plurals: compound nouns

A **compound noun** is one in which two or more words are joined, sometimes with hyphens. Confusion may arise concerning the position of the *s* in the **plural** form.
The *s* is added to the 'main' noun:

ex-husbands	Not **exs-husbands*
hair cuts	Not **hairs cut*
mothers-in-law	Not **mother-in-laws*
passers-by	Not **passer-bys*

In cases where there is no 'main' noun, the *s* is added to the end:
  cul-de-sacs/grown-ups/take-overs/etc.

point of view

The phrase **from my point of view** does not mean 'in my opinion'. The meaning is closer to 'from my position in life':
  From a student's point of view, the introduction of more exams is a bad idea.

politic/political

(1) **Politic** is a little-used word meaning 'wise' or 'prudent':
  a politic decision/advice/ etc.

(2) **Political** means 'pertaining to politics':
  a political party/prisoner/ etc.

practicable/practical

These words are frequently confused.

(1) **Practicable** means 'that may be practised, carried out, accomplished':

I do not think that educating our children at home is really practicable.

When referring to roads, it means 'passable':
Is this bridge practicable for heavy lorries?

(2) **Practical** can also be used in the sense of 'that may be practised, carried out' etc. However, the more usual sense is the opposite of 'theoretical':
I prefer practical medicine to studying from books.

A **practical** person is 'efficient in action':
I wish I was practical; I cannot even change a wheel on my car.

practice/practise
One of the most common errors in written English is to confuse the spelling of these two words. **Practice** is a noun, and **practise** is a verb.

precede   see **proceed**.

prefer
(1) When **prefer** is used with a noun, it is followed by *to*, not *than*:
She prefers classical music to jazz.

(2) When **prefer** is used with the infinitive of a verb, it is followed by **rather than**:
She prefers to cook rather than (to) go to restaurants.

preferable
It is not correct to use *more preferable* or *most preferable*:
Travelling by car is preferable to travelling by bus.

preoccupied
This word is followed by the preposition *with*, not *by*:
He is preoccupied with finding a new flat.

presume/assume
These words are not synonymous.
(1) **Presume** is used to mean 'a belief based on facts or probable evidence':
I heard the weather forecast for tomorrow, and we can presume it will not rain.

(2) **Assume** is used to mean 'take as the basis of argument' (ie with little concrete evidence):

> *Shall we assume it will not rain tomorrow, and plan the barbecue?*

principal/principle

These words are probably the most frequently confused pair in written English.

(1) **Principal** is both a noun and an adjective. The noun can mean 'the head of a school, college or university'. It can also mean 'money on which interest is paid'.

As an adjective, **principal** means 'most important':

> *The principal aim of this project is to create jobs.*

(2) **Principle** is a noun which means 'a rule of action' or 'a theoretical basis':

> *As a matter of principle, he never votes.*
> *What is the principle of nuclear energy?*

privilege

Note the spelling: there is no *d*.

proceed/precede

Be careful not to confuse these words: pay particular attention to the spelling.

(1) To **proceed** means 'to go on' or 'to begin and go on':

> *He proceeded to lecture us on the dangers of boxing.*
> *How shall I proceed with the experiment?*

(2) To **precede** is 'to go before':

> *At university, he preceded her by four years.*
> *The preceding entry in this book is* **privilege.**

professor/profession

These words are often misspelt. Remember: one *f* and double *s*.

program/programme

Traditionally, the British spelling of this word was **programme**, and the American, **program**. However, in the context of computers, the form **program** is now used in British English.

prone   see **apt.**

pronunciation

Note the spelling in the middle: the verb is **pronounce** but the noun is **pronunciation**.

prophecy/prophesy

Note that the noun is spelt *cy*, but the verb is spelt *sy*.

propose see **attempt**.

punctuation see individual entries.

purposely/purposefully

Be careful not to confuse these words.

(1) **Purposely** means 'intentionally':

He purposely arrives late, to annoy everyone.

(2) **Purposefully** means 'directed towards a purpose' or 'in a determined manner':

The teacher walked purposefully towards the children who were smoking.

Q

questionnaire

Note the spelling: double *n*.

quite   see **fairly**.

quiz

The plural of **quiz** is spelt with a double *z:* **quizzes**.

quotation marks

(1)   **Quotation marks,** also known as **inverted commas,** are used in the following ways:

(a)   To quote speech:

Double or single **quotation marks** may be used, although single ones are preferred in modern usage:

'What did you say?', asked Gerry.

(b)   To highlight a particular word or phrase:

Single **quotation marks** are usually used:

What does 'bonjour' mean?

However, if the highlighted word or phrase is part of a quote, we use the type not previously used:

'What does "mañana" mean?', asked Francine.

"What does 'mañana' mean?", asked Francine.

(2)   The use of other punctuation marks with **quotation marks** can cause uncertainty. The rules are:

(a)   Punctuation marks which belong to the quotation go inside the **quotation marks,** with commas before and/or after the reporting clause:

'I totally, and absolutely, refuse', he shouted, 'to continue!'

He whispered, 'Did you hear that noise?'

(b)   When a quote ends with a full stop which is not at the end of a complete sentence, the full stop is replaced by a comma:

'I do not care,' is what she finally replied.

(c)   When the quote ends with a full stop (or other punctuation mark) which is also at the end of the sentence, a second full stop is not added:

He said: 'I do not think so.'

Not **He said: 'I do not think so.'.*

She said, 'Leave me in peace!'

Not **She said, 'Leave me in peace!'.*

R

raise/rise

(1) **Raise, raised, raised**
Raise means 'to make higher':

> *The supermarket is always raising its prices.*

(2) **Rise, rose, risen**
Rise means 'to increase':

> *Prices are always rising.*

rather   see **fairly**.

rather than

In written English, when **rather than** is followed by a pronoun (I/me, he/him, etc) take care that the correct pronoun is used.

Rather than may be followed by subject pronouns (I, he, she, etc), or object pronouns (me, him, her, etc), depending upon the sentence.

Compare:

> *It was you, rather than she, who won the prize.*

Not **... rather than her*, because *you* and *she* are the subjects of the verb *won*.

> *I gave it to you rather than her.*

Not **... rather than she*, because *you* and *her* are the objects of the verb *give*.

reason

In correct English, **reason** should not be used with *why* or *because*:

> *The reason she did not marry him is a mystery.*
> Not **The reason why she did not ...*
> *The reason she did not marry him is that he did not want children.*
> Not **The reason she did not marry him is because he did not ...*

-re/-er   see **American spelling**.

receipt

Often misspelt. Note the vowels *ei*, and the *p* before *t*.

recommend

Do not confuse the *c* and the *m*: one *c*, but two *m*'s.

reconnaissance

Frequently misspelt. Note the double *n*'s and *s*'s in the middle, separated by *ai*.

refute/deny

These two words are often confused: **refute** is frequently used when **deny** would be more accurate.

(1) **Refute** means 'to disprove' (ie with evidence):
He refuted her allegations by showing documentary evidence of his innocence.

(2) **Deny** means 'to declare not to be true':
He denied her allegations but had no evidence to support his denial.

regard

(1) There is often confusion about whether or not to use an additional *s*:
With regard to; **in regard to**; and **as regards** are all correct in formal English.

(2) **Regard to** and **regard for** have different meanings.
Regard to means 'concerning':
With regard to yesterday, we shall say nothing further.
Regard for means 'concern, care, respect':
He has great regard for his father-in-law.

relation/relative

In the sense of 'related by blood or marriage' both **relation** and **relative** are correct.

rent   see **hire**.

replace/substitute

These words are often used incorrectly. Note the prepositions: **replace by/with** and **substitute for**.

(1) When **replace** is active, it is followed by **with**:
When Bill's car broke down, the car hire company replaced it with another one.

(2) When **replace** is passive, it is followed by **by**:
Bill's original car was replaced by another one.

However, if the 'agent' is mentioned (in this case, the car hire company), this changes to:

> *His original car was replaced by the company, with another one.*

(3) **Substitute** is followed by **for**:

> *The car hire company substituted another car for Bill's original one.*

request

To **request** means 'to ask for', and therefore **to* **request** *for* something is not correct.

rhyme/rhythm

Remember the *h* after the *r*.

rise   see **raise**.

S

scarcely   see **hardly**.

sceptic   see **cynic**.

schedule
Note the spelling: *s* and then *ch*.

Scottish/Scots/Scotch
These three words are often confused.
(1) **Scottish** is the usual adjective with the meaning 'of or belonging to Scotland':
She is Scottish; a Scottish university; a Scottish festival; etc.

(2) A person from Scotland is a **Scot**:
Many Scots have emigrated to Australia.
How many Scotsmen play football?

Scots is also the adjective usually used to describe the law and language of Scotland:
Scots law is different from English law.

(3) **Scotch** is an adjective often used to describe products or supposed products of Scotland:
Scotch whisky, Scotch terrier, Scotch egg, etc.
People from Scotland prefer not to be called **Scotch**.

-se   see **-ce**.

-sede   see **-cede**.

semicolon
There is often confusion about when a **semicolon** should be used.
(1) A **semicolon** may be used in lists, instead of a **comma**. This is usual when the items in a list need to be subdivided into groups, or when the list consists of long clauses (perhaps containing **commas**):
I want you to: phone Mr Ashling and arrange an appointment for next week; type these contracts, show them to Michael, and then post them; file those reports; ....

(2) A **semicolon** may be used instead of a **full stop,**

where two clauses are grammatically independent, but closely related in meaning:

> *The opera is well worth seeing; although it is expensive, I am going to see it again.*

separate

Frequently misspelt: one *e* at the beginning, one *e* at the end, and the vowels in the middle are *a*'s.

septic

Be careful not to confuse this word with *sceptic*. **Septic** means 'full of, or caused by, germs that are poisoning the blood':

> *a septic cut/poisoning/ etc.*

sergeant

A frequently misspelt word. Note the vowels: one *e* at the beginning, and *ea* later.

shall/will

There is some confusion about when **shall** and **will** should be used. One reason for this is that in spoken English, it is impossible to know which is being used, as the contracted forms of **shall** and **will** are the same:

> *I'll, he'll, etc.*

(1) **Shall** is used with **I** and **we** in the following cases:

  (a) in the simple future tense. **Will** is also correct, but formal English prefers **shall**:

> *Phone me tomorrow as I shall have more details then.*
> *If we miss the bus, we shall be late.*

  (b) with offers:

> *Shall I make you a cup of tea?*

  (c) with suggestions:

> *Shall we go to the park?*

  (d) with requests for instructions or advice:

> *What shall I do about it?*

In all other cases, **will** is used.

(2) In formal English, **shall** is used with other persons (not **I** or **we**), to express strong intentions, threats, or promises:

They shall never enter this house again.
If you do that again, he shall report you to the committee.
You shall have a watch, if you pass the exam.

In all other cases, **will** is used.

For **shall/will** in reported speech, see **should/would**.

should/would

There are two main areas of confusion concerning the use of **should** and **would**.

(1) Conditional sentences

In conditional structures (ie with *if*), both **should** and **would** can be used with **I/we,** although **should** is preferred in a formal style. With other persons, only **would** is correct:

If I won the lottery, I should never work again.
If he were richer, he would give up his job.

(2) Reported speech

When direct speech is reported, the tenses usually change. There is often uncertainty concerning how **shall** ought to change.

(a) When **shall** is used for suggestions, offers, or requests for advice/instructions, **shall** is usually changed to **should:**

Shall I help her?
He asked whether he should help her.
What shall we do with the dog, when we go on holiday?
She wanted to know what they should do with the dog, when they went on holiday.

(b) When **shall** is used to ask for information, it changes to **will/would**:

Shall I be in time for the train, if I leave here at 6pm?
He wants to know if he will be in time for the train if he leaves at 6pm.
Shall we have enough money to pay the bills?
She asked if they would have enough money to pay the bills.

(c) Normally a verb such as **shall** would be changed to its past tense, **should,** in reported speech. However, because **should** has several meanings (such as 'ought to'),

shall is usually changed to **would**, to avoid any ambiguity.

Compare:

I shall leave next week. (Future intention)

He said he should leave the following week. (Intention or obligation?)

He said he would leave the following week. (Intention)

singular/plural

(1) When two nouns are joined with *and*, and also used as the subject of the sentence, the verb is usually plural:

My son and daughter are both students.

(2) However, when the two nouns refer to a singular subject, the verb should be singular:

Fish and chips is my favourite food.

slander   see **libel**.

small/little

These words are not always interchangeable.

(1) When referring to a small size due to age, **little** is used:

a little boy etc.

(2) When expressing a feeling, as well as commenting on size, only **little** is correct:

She lives in a pretty little house in the country.

Poor little dog! Where is its owner?

so/therefore

Avoid using **so therefore** in written English; one or the other is sufficient:

I was hungry so I made a sandwich.

She was late for the meeting and therefore missed the director's speech.

sometime/some time

(1) **Sometime** means 'at a time not fixed':

I will phone you sometime next week.

(2) **Some time** means 'a little time':

There is still some time before the deadline.

speak to/with

Both forms are acceptable in British English, although **speak to** is more common. **Speak with** is more usual in American English.

special(ly)   see **especial(ly)**.

split infinitive

A **split infinitive** is where another word, or phrase, is put between **to** and the rest of the **infinitive**:

He likes to only speak German in Germany.

This construction receives great criticism and should be avoided where possible.

However, on some occasions a **split infinitive** is necessary in order to express the meaning clearly, or to give the desired emphasis to the verb.

Compare:

I want you to really like him. (ie to like him a lot)

I really want you to like him. (ie I want it a lot)

spontaneous

Note the spelling: *eous* at the end.

stationary/stationery

Two words which are frequently confused in writing.

(1) **Stationary** means 'unmoving':

a stationary bus, etc.

(2) **Stationery** means 'the goods sold by a stationer':

paper, envelopes, etc.

statistics

(1) The word **statistics** is used with a singular verb when referring to the academic subject:

Statistics is a very rewarding subject to study.

(2) When **statistics** refers to 'a collection of numerical data', it is used with a plural verb:

These statistics on unemployment are hard to believe.

The same applies to **mathematics**.

story/storey

(1) In the sense of a floor or a building, both spellings are correct. **Storey** is more common.

(2) **Story** is the only correct spelling for a tale or a narrative.

subject/verb agreement

(1) In English it is necessary to ensure that the *subject* and the *verb* agree, ie that both are plural, or that both are singular:

> *The advice of her teachers, parents, and friends, was needed to convince her to stay on at school.*
> Not *...were needed...*
> *A box of rotten apples was thrown away.*
> Not *...were thrown away.*

(2) Note that expressions referring to quantities, amounts, etc, usually have a singular verb as we view them as a single unit:

> *Six dollars is a lot to pay for that.*
> *Another five weeks seems a long time to wait.*
> *Every 2km there was another signpost.*

(3) Errors are often made with expressions using: *each, either, kind of, neither, none.* See individual entries for details.

(4) Some words, such as *group, family* and *committee,* may be singular or plural, depending upon the context. For details, see **group**.

subsequent   see **consequent**.

suffer

The preposition used after **suffer** is *from*, not *with*:

> *He suffers from asthma.*

superior

When **superior** means 'better' or 'higher in rank' it is followed by *to*, not *than*:

> *I do not like teachers who think they are superior to their students.*

swap/swop

Both of these spellings are correct, but **swop** is now more common than **swap**.

T

-t see **-ed**.

take/bring

These words are often used incorrectly.

(1) **Bring** is normally used to describe movement towards the speaker:

Bring me an apple, please.

Take is used for movements in other directions:

I am late for work: can you take the children to school?

(2) In letters, however, **bring** is used for movements towards both the reader and the writer.

Take is used for other directions:

When you come for the weekend, could you remember to bring your camera? I took mine on holiday and lost it...

Thanks for your letter. Of course I will bring my camera when I come.

This applies to all situations where the people communicating are in different places (eg on the phone).

tall/high

(1) **Tall** is used for people, trees, animals, buildings, and other things which are bigger in height than breadth:

chimneys/towers/giraffes/etc.

Tall is not used for things which are joined to anything at the top:

*Tall legs is incorrect.

(2) **High** means 'reaching far up' or 'far from a base' eg the ground:

high mountain/shelf/ etc.

than

(1) In comparisons, formal English prefers the use of subject pronouns (I, he, she, we, they) after **than**:

He is taller than I. (Not **than me.*)

We travel more than they. (Not **than them.*)

However, the use of *him/her* rather than *he/she* is becoming more common, even in a relatively formal style:

> *He is more nervous than her.*

(2) When the clause continues with a verb, the subject pronoun must be used:

> *She had more clothes than he did.* (Not *than him did.*)

These rules also apply to: *as, but,* and *except.*

their   see **they're**.

theirs/there's

When writing, take care not to confuse these words.

(1) **Theirs** is a possessive pronoun:

> *Whose is that car? It is theirs.*

(2) **There's** is the contracted form of *there is*. Note that contractions should not be used in formal written English.

therefore   see **so**.

there's   see **theirs**.

they/he or she

In informal English, **they, their,** and **them** are often used with a singular meaning, to avoid specifying the sex of the person, or people, referred to:

> *Has everyone got their book?*
> *If anyone wants me, tell them I will be back at 3pm.*

This use of **they** etc is becoming increasingly acceptable in a formal style. However, the traditional form is **he**, **his**, or **him**, to avoid the awkward **he or she**, **his or her**, etc:

> *Has everyone done his best?*
> *When a person is very stubborn, he can be difficult to work with.*

they're/their

Take care not to confuse these words in written English.

(1) **They're** is the contracted form of *they are*. Contractions should not be used in formal written English.

(2) **Their** is a possessive adjective:

> *Is this their car?*

though   see **although**.

till   see **until**.

try and/try to
   Try and... is often found in informal English. However, in a formal style, **try to...** is preferred:

> *Try to finish it this week.*
> *I will try to help him.*

tsar   see **czar**.

U

un-   see **in-**.

uninterested/disinterested

These words are not synonymous.

Uninterested means 'not taking an interest', while **disinterested** means 'impartial':

A judge should be disinterested in, but not uninterested in, a case.

unlike   see **like**.

unnatural/unnecessary/unnoticed

Note the double *n* in these words. When the prefix **un-** is added to words beginning with *n*, both *n*'s are retained.

unreadable   see **illegible**.

until/till

Although these words are synonymous, **until** is preferred in formal English. Take care with the spelling: **until** has only one *l*.

upward(s)   see **forward**.

used to

In the sense of past habits, **used to** has several correct forms in negatives and questions.

(1) Formal style:
    Used he to visit her regularly?
    He used not to be so argumentative.

(2) Neutral style:
    Did he use(d) to ride a motorbike?
    She didn't use(d) to like dogs.

W

was/were   see **if**.

weights and measures
These are often written incorrectly.
(1) The singular form is written before a noun:
a six-foot man
a four-kilo chicken
a two-litre bottle

(2) The plural form is used after the noun:
The man is six feet tall.
The chicken weighs four kilos.
The bottle holds two litres.

were   see **if**.

whatever/what ever   see **ever**.

whenever/when ever   see **ever**.

while/whilst
In modern English, **whilst** has been replaced by **while**, except in a very formal context.

whiskey/whisky
(1) **Whiskey** is the correct spelling of the drink made in Ireland. It is also the usual spelling in the USA.

(2) The usual British spelling is **whisky**, referring to the drink made in Scotland.

whoever/who ever   see **ever**.

who/whom
There is a great deal of uncertainty about when the pronouns **who** and **whom** should be used.
In questions, **who** is generally preferred, with **whom** only used in very formal English:
Who did they meet?
Whom did they promote?

Who

(1) **Who** is used when it is the subject of the following verb:

> *That is Tom, who won the marathon last year.* (**Who** refers to Tom, and he is the subject of the verb: *Tom won...*)
> *I think I saw the woman who stole the coat.* (**Who** refers to the woman, and she is the subject of the verb: *she stole...*)

(2) In a neutral style, **who** can be used with a preposition, like this:

> *There is the secretary who I spoke to.*
> *Who did he buy that coat for?*

Note: the preposition must come at the end of the clause.

Whom

(1) **Whom** is used when it is the object of the following verb:

> *I think I saw the woman whom the detective described.*
> (**Whom** refers to the woman, and she is the object of the verb: *the detective described her.*)
> *This is Mr Smithies, whom you interviewed last year.*
> (**Whom** refers to Mr Smithies, and he is the object of the verb: *you interviewed him.*)

This structure is quite formal; in informal English **whom** would be replaced by **who**.

(2) After prepositions **whom** should be used:

> *There is the secretary to whom I spoke yesterday.*
> *For whom did he buy that?*

This is quite formal; for a less formal style see **who**.

who's/whose

(1) **Who's** is the contracted form of *who is* and *who has*:

> *David is the only one who's getting a prize.*
> *Who's been sleeping in my bed?*

Contractions are not acceptable in formal written English.

(2) **Whose** refers to possession:

> *That is the man whose wife had quadruplets.*

why   see **reason**.

wide   see **broad**.

will   see **shall**.

win/beat

These are often used incorrectly.

One **wins** a game, an argument, a prize, etc. One **beats** the person, team, etc, that one is playing, arguing against, etc:

> *He won the game of chess.*
> *He beat Nigel at chess.*

would   see **should**.

X Y

-xion   see **-ction**.

yacht
> Note the spelling: *ch* before *t*.

yoghurt/yoghourt/yogurt
> These are all correct spellings, but the most common form is **yoghurt.**

your/you're
> These are often written incorrectly.
> (1) **Your** is a possessive adjective:
>   *Is this your bag?*
>
> (2) **You're** is the contracted form of *you are*:
>   *You're going now, aren't you?*
> Contracted forms are not acceptable in formal writing.

Yours faithfully/sincerely   see **letter writing**.